AF130763

Judith Zylla-Woellner

Quota for women in management positions?

An analysis of the implementation of the women's quota in Germany

Anchor Academic
Publishing

Zylla-Woellner, Judith: Quota for women in management positions? An analysis of the implementation of the women's quota in Germany. Hamburg, Anchor Academic Publishing 2013

Buch-ISBN: 978-3-95489-090-3
PDF-eBook-ISBN: 978-3-95489-590-8
Druck/Herstellung: Anchor Academic Publishing, Hamburg, 2013

Bibliografische Information der Deutschen Nationalbibliothek:
Die Deutsche Nationalbibliothek verzeichnet diese Publikation in der Deutschen Nationalbibliografie; detaillierte bibliografische Daten sind im Internet über http://dnb.d-nb.de abrufbar.

Bibliographical Information of the German National Library:
The German National Library lists this publication in the German National Bibliography. Detailed bibliographic data can be found at: http://dnb.d-nb.de

© Anchor Academic Publishing, Imprint der Diplomica Verlag GmbH
Hermannstal 119k, 22119 Hamburg
http://www.diplomica-verlag.de, Hamburg 2013
Printed in Germany

List of Contents

ABSTRACT

In 1949 the German constitution set down the entitlement to equality for men and women in the Federal Republic of Germany in article 3. Until the late 1950s it was up to men to decide where to live and how to utilise families' assets. Women were not permitted to decide about their participation in the labour market but had the duty to administer the household and help their husband. When Angela Merkel became chancellor of Germany in 2005, she was not only one of the most influential politicians in the world but also one of the few female leaders who managed to break through the glass ceiling.

Chancellor Merkel herself blocked Minister of Employment, Ursula von der Leyens attempt towards affirmative action. The fact of the matter is that Germany is lagging behind when it comes to women in leading positions. In 2010, only 0,9% of the leadership positions in the 100 largest German companies and 2,6% in the top 200 companies are held by women. (Holst & Wiemer, 2010) This is in stark contrast with the fact that at team-leader level in German companies, women represent 20% of staff after being almost 60% of university graduates.

This underrepresentation is especially difficult to understand since recent studies have shown a positive correlation between the proportion of women in management positions and companies' performance, which made approximately 10% more in terms of profits with a balanced gender policy (Wiemer, 2010).

As a consequence, Germany is facing a discussion on the introduction of a women's quota for management positions in German companies. Currently there is a great debate on-going concerning the pros and cons of a women's quota.

"More women in leadership positions are not a mandate of misunderstood egalitarianism. It's a requirement of social fairness."

René Obermann, CEO of Deutsche Telekom

1. Introduction

In 1949 the German Constitution set down the entitlement to equality for men and women in the Federal Republic of Germany in article 3. Until the late 1950s it was up to men to decide where to live and how to utilise families' assets. Women were not permitted to decide about their participation in the labour market but had the duty to administer the household and help their husband.

In 1977, paragraph 75 of the Industrial Constitutional Law finally legislated for gender equality in working life, without any gender specific regulation regarding domestic duties. (Holst & Wiemer, 2010) While women's partaking in the paid workforce is one of the most meaningful changes in the past 50 years, men nevertheless occupy 70% of top managerial positions. Traditional abilities and stereotypes still hinder women from reaching the top and encourage them to rather take up part time positions, which reconcile work and family obligations. (Rindfleish & Sheridan, 2003)

Germany, being ranked number 13 of the European countries by having 25% females in managerial positions, clarifies that it is still far from having attained equality for women in leading positions. (Kommission, 2011)

When Angela Merkel became chancellor of Germany in 2005, she was not only one of the most influential politicians in the world but also one of the few female leaders who managed to break through the glass ceiling. In 2006 she was voted the most powerful woman by Time Magazine and has held the position of Chancellor for two electoral terms now. Despite the fact that an East German woman leads Germany and there are five female ministers out of a total of sixteen, the political situation is not reflected in German businesses. The fact of the matter is that chancellor Merkel herself blocked Minister of Employment Ursula von der Leyen's attempt towards affirmative action, declaring: (...) there will be no legally mandated quota for women in Germany."

But the question is, will Germany, without a quota, be able to face the shortage of skilled labour a few years from now, resulting from the already declining birth rates and the growth of the elderly generation? All these issues could cause the German economy, aligned with the German welfare, to collapse, if politicians and economy do not start working together and utilise the hidden potential offered by fine erudite women.

"No society can afford to simply ignore 50 per cent of its potential."
Karen Duve, Author

1.2. Background & Cause for Interest

The primary intention of this thesis will be to outline the situation Germany is currently facing in terms of women in top managerial positions as well as the difficulty of reunification of family and working life.

The fact of the matter is that Germany is lagging behind when it comes to women in leading positions. In 2010, only 0,9% of the leadership positions in the 100 largest German companies and 2,6% in the top 200 companies are held by women. (Holst & Wiemer, 2010) This is in stark contrast with the fact that at team-leader level in German companies' women represent 20% of staff after being almost 60% of university graduates.

This underrepresentation is especially difficult to understand since recent studies have shown a positive correlation between the proportion of women in management positions and company's performance, which made approximately 10% more in terms of profits with a balanced gender policy (Wiemer, 2010).

As a consequence, Germany is facing a discussion about the introduction of a women's quota for management positions in German companies. Some German politicians are especially keen on introducing the women quota in German companies aligned with a child-care program offered by the government. Currently there is a great debate on-going on the pros and cons of a women's quota.

Germany also finds itself under a lot of pressure by the European Union due to European Commissioner for Justice, Fundamental Rights and Citizenship Viviane Reding's assertion that the voluntary women's quotas in businesses have failed.

It is worth pointing out that there are no German companies among the 24 signatories of the voluntary agreement. The voluntary agreement stipulates that the number of women in top positions should be at 30% by 2015 and 40% by 2020. (Spiegel Online, 2012)

Germany is also facing a shortage of skilled personnel and qualified junior staff. Getting more women into qualified jobs could be one solution to the demographic challenges of the future. Therefore, this thesis will discuss the issue of the male monoculture in top management.

"An equal participation of women and men in decision-making processes is a democratic and economic necessity. In the current economic situation it is all the more important to mobilise all talents. This is not the time to waste skills and production potential because of out-dated perceptions of women's and men's roles and leadership abilities." (European-Commission, 2010, p. 13)

„We are, at present, regarding women in leadership positions, on one level with India but behind Russia, Brazil and China."
Ursula von der Leyen, Minister of Employment

1.3. RELEVANCE FOR GERMANY

In 2010 only 3,2 % of places on German executive boards were filled by women - male representatives took all other board seats. In comparison, seven years earlier Norway introduced a quota stipulating a minimum of 40% women in supervisory boards. This goal was achieved in 2009.

During the very same time period Germany has not significantly increased the percentage of women in supervisory board. It is striking to find Germany last with India in an international ranking regarding percentage of women in executive boards, behind Sweden, USA, UK, Norway, Russia, China, France, Spain, and Brazil. (Holst & Schimeta, 2011)

This status quo is very worrying since Germany is not in the position to not use the human capital offered through women. Due to demographic changes, Germany faces a severe shortage of skills, which will continue and will reach a peak in 2020 with a need for 29% additional academic skilled labour. A study done by McKinsey & Company predicts a decrease of the labour force in Europe by 24m by 2036, if the female labour quota does not increase. Providing European countries do implement policies to increase the female labour force; the decrease of the general labour strength is only anticipated to be minus 3m. (McKinsey, 2007)

Even more striking is the fact that women, who on average achieve better grades in school and university degrees than men, receive more than half of the university entrance diplomas. (Holst, 2008) The Federal Statistical Office measured 51,1% female graduates in 2010. In Germany women also comprise approximately 60% of all business graduates from German universities. (Moore, 2010)

These numbers do not match women's participation in economic leading positions. Despite their high educational achievements, women have difficulty entering leadership positions and breaking the glass ceiling, especially when they try to have a family. This is why many politicians and social scientists see the necessity of more women in leading positions and consequently demand the women quota. In 2010 the German party "Die Grünen" drafted a bill suggesting a minimum percentage of 40% for gender balance executive boards. As of now, the bill was not approved and did not receive a majority in the German Bundestag. (Holst & Wiemer, 2010)

So far, no political affirmative action has been implemented nor was voluntary commitment of companies successful. Consequently the European Union is putting pressure on German companies and European Commissioner for Justice Viviane Reding is losing patience: "I am not a fan of quotas. However I like the results they bring." (Thornton, 2012)

She asks for a voluntary commitment of companies to introduce more women to top jobs – 30 per cent until 2015 and 40 per cent until 2020. Until 2012 only 24 European Companies signed with no German company among them. (Spiegel Online, 2012)

4

2. RESEARCH AIM & OBJECTIVES

Getting to grasp with the initial position, the author will try to find an answer whether a binding quota for women is the right path for Germany.

Before dealing with the main questions, several other research questions will need to be tackled:

Is there a leadership style that differentiates men and women? - Based on the transactional & transformational leadership style?

Why are there fewer women in top managerial positions in Germany?

What should be done and are there certain measures that help women to break through the glass ceiling in Germany?

Is the women's quota the most effective and sustainable way to get more women in top leadership positions in Germany?

The thesis will comprise of three main parts:

Firstly, the author will give an overview of transactional and transformational leadership theories, juxtaposing them and finding the relevant aspects for women in leading positions.

In the second part, the status quo of working women in Germany will be investigated. There are various studies by consulting groups and the German Department of Employment and the European Union that offer up to date data and statistics concerning this issue. Using that secondary data, the author would like to paint a realistic picture of the challenges for politics and economy. Furthermore will that chapter explore how men and women perceive the situation.

The author will also have a look at processes accompanying the women's furtherance as well as the negative impact the quota could have on economy and society. The findings of that analysis will help to answer the questions of the why there are fewer women in management positions and what measures need to be implemented to ensure that more women rise into leadership positions.

The third and final part will be a summary of the prior aspects and a more focused look at Germany. What exact measures could be introduced in Germany in order to get more women in managerial positions and is the advertised women's quota a realistic and sustainable concept for Germany.

The author will close the paper with a critical discussion of the quota and outline feasible suggestions to get more women into top positions.

These research questions and objectives will lead to the main research question tackled by the thesis:

➜ *Quota for women in management positions? - An analysis of the implementation and necessity of the women's quota in Germany following the guidance of other European countries.*

The author will try to generate an ideal and theoretic compendium of methods, approaches and tools of how to get more women in leading positions. The dissertation aims to give an idea of whether political regulation is beneficial or if other measures could have the same effect being more feasible.

2.1. METHODOLOGICAL APPROACH

The basis for this master thesis will be secondary data mainly consisting of studies by the German government, the European Union and consultancy firms. Moreover, the author has also reviewed the relevant scientific journals and related literature. Also recent Internet articles and reports were used, because the women quota is highly topical in Germany. This was also necessary to grasp current opinions and latest changes within the country and the European Union. The author relied on secondary data because this topic is well researched and a lot has been written about it. Moreover, secondary literature gives an excellent overview of the topic, which could have not been accomplished by personal extensive research.

Primary data collected by the author was also not an option due to time constraints of only three month for completion for the thesis. For some primary data/opinion, the author conducted one additional interview with a female managing director in Germany. The reason for choosing that interview partner for the thesis was firstly her current position as business leader of one of the top private universities in Germany. Secondly her international working experience and her comparison of working environments for women made her an interesting candidate for an interview. Lastly she is a working mother, embodying the target group this thesis is about.

The author anticipates some methodological limitations - especially concerning the data comparison. Since the data comes from different sources with various reasons for interest as well as different time frames, the international comparison of key numbers proved to be difficult. Also the analysis was challenging due to changing figures as well as missing data of key countries. Furthermore the interpretation and definition of data varied depending on the source.

Thus the suggestion of the author would be to continue and enhance international and European data collection, especially since certain countries do have the quota while others do not. It would be especially interesting to see the long-term development of such countries. Another hindrance and thus room for improvement would be a mutual definition of leadership denotation and terms.

Due to the different approaches and questionnaire participants, a clear statement is problematic. For instance, the position of managers, executive managers, heads, boards members, executives, leaders, etc. mean different positions in individual companies and countries. Thus the application of the issue as well as the quota regulation proved to be challenging.

2.2. RESEARCH DESIGN

The reasoning of the thesis will be based on inductive methodology. The paper will open with leadership theories related to the topic, followed by an analysis of available statistical data from Germany, trying to find a tailored answer and tools for Germany handling the women quota.

Therefore one can say that the overall research design will be analytic and a mixture of qualitative and quantitative data. The quantitative data will be primarily measure the performance of German businesses, draw conclusions and analyse the need for a women's quota. The qualitative data is an important tool to use, reflect and comprehend the desire and need for more women in management positions.

Qualitative facts are essential to give an idea about a very opinionated issue, which involves society, economy and politics and cannot be merely reflected by just presenting quantitative data. The mixed method of qualitative and quantitative approach has proved to be an excellent tool, reasoning the introduction of the women's quota and still include all parameters. The combination of figures and statements make the analysis within the thesis comprehensive and thorough.

The goal of the inductive approach will be to find specific answers for the underrepresented women situation in German companies.

2.3. LITERATURE REVIEW

The literature sources regarding leadership theory are endless and publications on leadership can be found in versatile selections of professional and practitioner journals comprising several disciplines such as management, psychology, sociology, political science, public administration as well as educational administration.

This paper will include literature and views from all these discipline since the topic of the women quota in leadership positions touches all of these fields.

Nevertheless the author has decided to focus solely on transformational and transactional leadership theory with regards to characteristics of a female leadership style.

Articles by Iain Hay as well as meta-analysis by the female social psychologists Alice Eagly and Blair Johnson on gender and leadership will base the theoretical discussion. Alice Eagly and Mary Johannesen-Schmidt also performed a study on the leadership styles of men and women, which will be discussed.

One advantage is that the findings from Hay and Eagly are reasonably new. Most leadership theories are more than 30 years old, when women did not play a great role in management positions as they do now. During the 1980's, research was done on charismatic, situational and transformational leadership. There is extensive literature, mostly by Eagly, on similarities of successful transformational leaders and female leadership styles.

Thus the theoretical literature concerning the topic can without difficulty relate to the pressing issue of leading women.

The literature regarding the current situation in Germany and the pressing question of the necessity to implement a quota will be mainly extracted from recent journal articles and daily reports.

Due to the rapid change of the German and world economy as well as political enforcement, the author needs to be up to date regarding the newest developments and opinions.

These precise circumstances have been shown to be more difficult, because the literature and news reports available are overwhelming but also redundant. Thus the author decided to rely mainly on one scientific source (DIW) and only little input through weekly online news magazines like Spiegel and Global Post. As the author knows that those sources are not comprehensive, the decision in favour was made due to the length of the thesis.

3. theoretical Framework

This thesis will discuss the possibility of a women quota in leadership positions in Germany. Therefore the theoretical discussion will comprise the concept of leadership theories particularly related to female leaders. The key idea is to investigate the possibility of a typical female leadership style. Furthermore one would like to examine if there are similarities between a particularly successful leadership style and characteristics of female leadership.

The rough definition of leadership is organizing a group of individuals and its processes of social influence to attain a shared goal or mutual endeavour. Leadership is a collective process shared among members of the group in which the leader usually has a formal authority and more influence. (Bolder, et al., 2003)

One can assume that leadership is as old as mankind and therefore the concept of leadership is discussed in a wide range of literature. Over time, different leadership concepts have been developed named mostly after their male contrivances: Adair's Action-Centred Leadership Model, Tannenbaum & Schmidt's Leadership Continuum, Hersey & Blanchard's Model of Leadership, Great man theory, trait theory, behavioural theory, Fielder's contingency theory and attribution theory.

All these theories have been developed over the past 70 years based on different approaches like who exerts influence, the purpose of influence attempts, and the way influence is exerted.

Then again, most leadership theories share principal components like vision, inspiration, role modelling, intellectual stimulation, meaning making, appeals to higher-order needs, empowerment, setting of high expectations and fostering collective identity. (Conger, 1999)

Yukl hits the mark: "(...) there are almost as many definitions of leadership as there are persons who have attempted to define the concept." (Yukl, 1989, p. 252)

But the core theoretical groundwork for this thesis will cover the **concept of transactional leadership versus transformational leadership theory**.

These opposing leadership styles are explained on the bases of the relationship between individuals and the level of exchange they have.

"This capacity to shape a vision of what can be achieved, and to share the vision with others so that it becomes their own, is one of the most important elements of leadership."

Professor David Pennington, Vice Chancellor of the University of Melbourne

3.1. TRANSACTIONAL VERSUS TRANSFORMATIONAL LEADERSHIP

Famous sociologists like Max Weber, Bernard Bass or McGregor Burns have done the most important research on transformation leadership. Burns advanced this theory mainly from descriptive research on political leaders and juxtaposes transformational leadership with transactional leadership. In Burns' opinion, leaders are not born nor made, but evolve from a structure of motivation, values and goals. In order to relate to the concept one must understand the essential differences between transactional and transformational leadership.

The basis for leadership is the relationship between two people, which again is maintained by the level of exchange between both. The greater the exchange between two individuals, of any kind – materialistic or non-materialistic, the stronger the relationship. (Stewart, 2006)

The transactional relation is based on requirements, conditions and rewards for efforts. (Bass, 2006)

For instance, if employees deliver good work they get a generous bonus in return. Leaders leading in this manner are called **transactional leaders**.

Accordingly managers know about the connection between the effort shown and reward given as well as use the standard measures of incentive, reward, punishment and sanction in order to control subordinates. These managers promise rewards for good performance and look out for unconventionalities from rules and standards applying corrective actions when necessary. Moreover, this style is more oriented to the present, only dealing with current issues. (Bass, 2006) To put it in a nutshell, the transactional motivation is done by setting goals and promising rewards for the expected performance.

"Transactional leadership is a prescription for mediocrity (...) intervening with his or her group only when procedures and standards for accomplishing tasks are not being met – If it ain't broken, don't fix it." (Bass, 2006, p. 20) A manager with this behaviour pattern uses disciplinary threats to get employees to perform, which is ineffective and in the long term counterproductive.

According to Eagly, men are more likely to be transactional leaders. Her findings suggest that male managers being transactional leaders paid attention to their follower's problems and mistakes, waited until problems became severe before attempting to solve them and were absent and uninvolved at critical time. (Eagly & Johannesen-Schmidt, 2001)

How these findings come along with transformational and female leaders will be discussed in the following passages.

Transformational leaders on the other hand are simply described by unconditional, dedicated and committed. They rather use empowerment than control strategies achieving influence over their employees. Transformational leaders influence major transformations in the attitudes and conventions of organisation members and build commitment for the companies mission, objectives and strategies. This kind of leadership can be observed on the micro level – relationships between individual; as well as the macro level – intention to change social systems and reform organisations. Those leaders also value ideals and morals such as liberty, justice, equality, peace and humanitarianism. (Yukl, 1989)

The irony is that this leadership style is metaphorically explained with a mother and her unconditional care for her kids. Related to working environment Hay describes the style as follows:

"(...) Occurs when leaders broaden and elevate the interest of their employees, when they generate awareness and acceptance of the purpose and mission of the group (...) transforma-tional leaders elevate people from low levels of need, focused on survival to higher levels (...) engender trust, admiration, loyalty and respect amongst their followers." (Hay, 2011, p. 3)

Transformational leaders are determined to reach a certain mutual goal and are an inspiration to their followers. This leadership kind also likes to develop employees, provide encourage-ment and takes over a mentoring task in order to promote individual growth opportunity. Following Bass: leaders transform followers making them more aware of the importance of their work and by encouraging them to surpass self-interest for the sake of the organisation. (Bass, 2006)

"Transformational leaders recognise and exploit an existing need to demand of a potential follower and look for potential motives in followers, seek to satisfy higher needs and engages the full person of the follower." (MacGregor Burns, 2003, p. 28)

Empirical data by Bass confirmed that there are four common dimensions of transformational leadership.

The first stage is:

1) Idealised Influence – The leader inspires subordinates with charismatic visions and behaviour.

2) Inspirational Motivation – The leader's ability to encourage others as well as to commit to the company's vision and follow a new idea. They encourage staff to become part of the organisation and its culture. Followers grow trust and respect towards the leader.

3) Intellectual Stimulation – The leader's capacity to inspire and encourage staff's innovation and creativity and see meaning in their work & accomplishments.

4) Individualised Consideration - The leader's skill in coaching subordinates and understanding their specific needs and talent. This also ensures that all followers are included in transformational organisational processes.

These key dimension lead to subordinate performances beyond the company's expectations. (Hay, 2011)

Graphic 1 – Characteristics of a Transformational Leader | Compare Bass 2006

Transformational leaders evoke emotions in their employees, who encourage them to go the extra mile and accomplish goals beyond their job description and own interest. Those leaders can be characterised (see graphic 1) by their pro-activeness, inspirational, intellectual stimulating, creating new learning opportunities and possessing good rhetorical and managerial skills. They are also likely to develop solid emotional but respective bonds with subordinates and are known for their motivational speeches as well as their spread of optimism. Transformational managers are pioneers of change, questioning traditions and standards, encouraging the team to enhance innovative and creative problems. (Hay, 2011) This manager type is also ready to give out words of praise and thanks, building their followers' self-confidence.

Bass brings the difference between both styles to a point: "(...) the transactional leader works within the organisation culture as it exists; the transformational leader changes the organisational culture" (Bass, 2006, p. 5)

Especially fast technological and global change as well as increasing competition from recently industrialised countries requires a significant organisational change within companies. The challenge for companies is to implement drastic change but not demoralise staff and hinder their work. According to the transformational leadership characteristics, transformational managers who guide organisational improvement, effectiveness and institutional cultural change can handle circumstances of change most sustainable. (Hay, 2011)

"Managers who behave like transformational leaders are more likely to be seen by their colleagues and employees as satisfying and effective leaders than those who behave like transactional leaders." (Bass, 2006, p. 21)

> *"Management positions are awarded based on contacts and continuity rather than as a result of qualifications and competence."*
> Anke Domscheit-Berg, Initiative for more Women in Board Positions

3.2. CRITICAL ASPECTS

Reflecting transformational theory, there are also some voices of criticism and doubt like: "the dark side of charisma". The major concern is that this leadership style has potential for abusing its power.

As transformational leaders evoke strong emotions beneath subordinates and have a powerful influence on them, trust and respect is easy to betray. Furthermore they can have the inclination to narcissism and manipulation. (Hall, et al., 2008)

"Transformational leadership lacks the checks and balances of countervailing interests, influence and power that might help to avoid dictatorship and oppression of a minority by a majority." (Hay, 2011, p. 13)

Critics refer to the danger of amoral self-promotion by managers caused by the practice of impression management. "They become actors seeking the next round of applause." (Conger, 1999, p. 172) Another danger is seen in motivating subordinates to go beyond their own self-interest and companies expectations, which cannot be handled by all employees and might lead towards socially unacceptable behaviour. Some employees are not capable of handling situations like that and rather just "do their job". Moreover, the numerous benefits ascribed to transformational leaders could be harmful by creating highly dependent individuals.

Thus moral foundations are crucial for both transformational leadership and leadership in general.

This issue is summed up in this quote to a core: "(...) to bring about change, authentic transformational leadership fosters the moral values of honesty, loyalty, and fairness, as well as the end values of justice, equality, and human right." (Griffin 2003, as cited in Hay, p. 11)

3.3. ARE THERE COMMONALITIES OF FEMALE AND TRANSFORMATIONAL LEADERSHIP STYLES?

In order to be an effective leader, one needs to influence employees in a positive way reaching the goals of an organisation. Learning from the characteristics, transformational leadership can help managers to become exceptional leaders. This form of leadership is also known as targeting the levels of motivation and innovation that is required in changing and exceeding competitive settings, which we are facing in today's world.

Research implies that female leaders come to transformational leadership naturally and inhabit characteristics and skills associated with that style. Subordinates observe more correspondence between leaders feminine personality attributes and transformational style. (Eagly & Johannesen-Schmidt, 2001)

"(...) Research indicates that the values and skills women were socialised to develop may be consistent with transformational leadership." (Druskat, 1994, p. 101)

Druskat summarises Goldberger's findings from a research project in the 1980s, where women related to their working environment, reported a strong commitment towards values and preferred connection over separation, understanding and acceptance over assessment, collaboration over competition and discussion over debate. (Druskat, 1994)

These findings mirror and are consistent with the characteristics of transformational and female leadership and are nourished by Eagly's findings on commonality of transactional leadership and male leadership styles.

According to Eagly, women are also more likely to encourage participation, share their power as well as information, enhance the self-esteem of others and energise employees. (Eagly & Johnson, 1990)

"In comparison to male leaders, women have been found to be more democratic, participative, more interpersonally oriented and less task oriented in certain situations." (Druskat, 1994, p. 103)

Although there is a lot of criticism on the thesis of women having specific transformational leadership behaviours, Druskat found proof for that presumption. "Both women and men leaders were rated to exhibit more transformational leadership behaviours than transactional

14

leadership behaviours. However, women leaders were rated to exhibit significantly more transformational behaviours than men leaders and male leaders were rated to exhibit significantly more transactional behaviours than women leaders." (Druskat, 1994, p. 114) These findings also put the exclusiveness of only women being transformational leaders into perspective. One could assume that leading transformational is so successful that there is a selectiveness of good leaders and therefore this style is more suitable at present and therefore more often represented by both women and men.

Nonetheless it seems inevitable that women incorporate the tendency to lead more transfor-mational by nature. " (…) In context where more women held power, women leaders displayed much more transformational than transactional leadership and were rated as more transfor-mational than male leaders in an all-male context. (…) Women leaders were better at meeting the desire and expectations for empathic, nurturing, person-centred leadership than the men leaders. Thus transformational leadership may require skills traditionally associated with women." (Druskat, 1994, p. 114 ff) Eagly's findings add: "(…) female managers, more than male managers, manifest attributes that motivate their followers to feel respect and pride by their association with them, show optimism and excitement about future goals and attempt to develop and mentor followers and attend to their individual needs." (Eagly & Johannesen-Schmidt, 2001, p. 15)

As mentioned in the introduction, vibrant times of economic change call for transformational leaders who guide motivation and innovation essential to compete. Women can take over this role; however companies must promote a culture where diversity is valued and transforma-tional management is fortified. Organisation can only benefit from an executive culture where both men and women can perform best.

"After years of analysing what makes leaders most effective and figuring out who's got the Right Stuff, management gurus now know how to boost the odds of getting a great execu-tive: Hire a female!"

Sharpe, Business Week

3.4. IS THERE A TYPICAL FEMALE LEADERSHIP STYLE?

Obvious biological sex differences cause men and women to be fairly different even if they inhabit the same management position. It seems to be common sense that women personify a typical way of leading employees which is different from men: less hierarchical, more coopera-tive and more oriented to boosting others self-worth. But is there really something like a typical female leadership behaviour? According to Alice Eagly and her conducted meta-analyses, women are ascribed to manners concerned with the welfare for others; for instance, affectionate, friendly, pleasant, helpful, kind, sympathetic, interpersonally, sensitive, nurturing and gentle behaviour. Regarding professional settings, these typical female behaviours show

15

themselves by: speaking hesitantly, not drawing attention to oneself, accepting others direction, supporting others and contributing to the resolution of relational issues. (Eagly & Johannesen-Schmidt, 2001)

Therefore Eagly argues that these gender roles and stereotypes spill over to organisations and are responsible for a background identity in the workplace. Furthermore she states that employees react to managers referring to their stereotyped expectations towards them and because they internalised well-known gender roles. This stereotype cultivation also creates a statistical discrimination within recruiting in companies and therefore barriers for women accessing management positions.

"As a consequence of these differing social identities, men and women have somewhat different expectations for their own behaviour in organisational setting. (…) Self-definition of managers may reflect a blending of their managerial role and gender role, and, through self-regulatory processes, these composite self-definitions influence behaviour. (…) People thus tend to have similar beliefs about leaders and men but dissimilar beliefs about leaders and women" (Eagly & Johannesen-Schmidt, 2001, p. 18 ff)

According to Deaux; major expectations and stereotypes in any situation can modify or stipulate leadership behaviour. Thus he claims that behaviour is determined by the expectations and choices of both the perceiver and the target, which is mainly influenced by the particular framework in which the interaction arises. Moreover Eagly alludes that communicating an expectation to a target can generate a self-fulfilling prophecy. (Druskat, 1994)

Other social scientists assert that female managers experience conflicts between their gender role and their leadership role, which creates a conflict because normative expectations of being a good leader are associated with more masculine than feminine qualities. (Eagly & Johnson, 1990) Hence managerial woman face pressure from two directions: following their gender role can mean failure to meet the expectations of their leader role and conforming to their leader role could mean failing the necessities of their gender role – family role. This problem (caused by society) means that women cannot succeed in both roles.

As for Eagly, gender roles spill over to organisational settings; at the same time leaders' gender identities may compel their behaviours in a direction dependent on their own gender role. One could assume that this is why women try to adapt male leadership behaviours and therefore be more accepted. "(…) because men have long held these leading roles, they have defined the styles to which people have become accustomed." (Eagly & Carli, 2003, p. 3)

To make matters even more difficult, Eagly's finding show that employees evaluate autocratic/transactional manners by females more negatively than they did the same behaviour by male leaders. Thus, women experience negative reactions by showing male leadership characteristics. (Eagly & Johannesen-Schmidt, 2001) This would mean that male leaders have the liberty to lead in a more autocratic manner and still being accepted, while women are in a lose-lose situation taking up an either female style or adopting male leadership characteristics. Unfortunately women's competence and ability to lead is often questioned and is accompanied by reluctant staff and a less supportive environment.

The easiest and maybe best and most natural way of leadership for women therefore seems to be transformational management, making collaborative decisions according to staff's expectations and consequently gaining trust and confidence.

If they develop their own inclusive features of management, they are more likely to defeat subordinates resistance, gain their approval and be more effective. This theory is also supported by Eagly's meta-analysis.

"Another reason that women fare better than men may be the tendency for the female gender role to foster more feminine styles. Thus, individualised consideration and to some extent, contingent reward may involve being attentive, considerate, and nurturing to ones subordinates, tendencies that are consistent with the female gender role. (…) Being supportive of subordinates may foster showing optimism and excitement about the future." (Eagly & Carli, 2003, p. S. 20)

In short, gender roles and labels are reasonably important influences on behaviour and tend to produce gender-stereotypic behaviour in the professional context. That is why the media likes to assume that women are better managers, because they try to perform better (to meet higher standards), consider the individual employee and therefore be more effective. (Eagly & Johannesen-Schmidt, 2001)

Another very practical advantage women or parents inhabit is; they are organisational talents. Others have to gain this experience by engaging in honorary, non- profit engagement but mothers especially are strong multitaskers, organisational geniuses, and pragmatic, resilient and familiar with resolving conflicts.

However, fast changing business environments demand a new breed of organisational frontrunners. The research results listed reveal that women may be appropriate to fill this void. This research also recommends that female managers should not change their leadership style to meet masculine standards and expectations of traditional organisations.

These finding are underpinned by Danna Jeschke and lead over to the next chapter: "Do not get frustrated with all the men. You can do both kids and career. Do not try to be perfect. Try to be good in your job and a good mom at home and everything will be fine. Do not try too hard. If you are too dynamic, people think you are too hard, if you are too soft you appear to be weak. One thing I learned is, that you should never try to adapt to male leadership styles. Be like you are, you do not have the energy to be somebody you are really not. Women care too much, but they are better leaders because they reflect." (Jeschke, 2012)

3.5. BETTER LEADERSHIP THROUGH WOMEN?

One question remains unanswered: Are women better leaders? In order to answer, one has to find out how a good leader or manager is defined: Specialised competence and skills, intelligence, ability to think analytically and willingness are the very basic requirements for managers. But there are abilities beyond these fundamental criteria that make good leaders employees like to follow.

Communicative competence is one additional criterion, which comprises listening to others, gaining information and giving feedback to superiors. Equally important is teamwork including interdisciplinary thinking and working.

A report by the OECD about gender and sustainable development in 2009 ascertains; " (...) that women managers bring a wider range of perspectives to bear in corporate decision-making, contribute team-building and communication skills, and help organisations to adapt to changing circumstances." (Holst & Wiemer, 2010)

The ability of a holistic approach, especially in projects, is becoming more important. Another vital factor is the ability to solve conflicts and tensions, making sure the team or department is working well. This also implies managing diversity, being accepting, flexible and sensitive handling gender, age, nationality and different ethnic groups. At the same time, excellent managers have to offer universal and systemic thinking as well as flexibility. In terms of dealing with diversity, managers not only have to have the language skills but also adapt intercultural management abilities. These days, business is facing fast changing, complex, sometimes-intangible circumstances that need to be handled efficiently and quickly. Managers have to deal with such issues skilfully, innovatively and flexibly. These changes also request leaders to be willing to obtain lifelong learning. Not only do they have to continuously study further but also be able to keep up with new technologies.

One last essential skill successful managers have to possess is replaying sense and vision, create values and be a good role model. (Henn, 2009) Screening these requirements, one can grasp how various the skills are and how only a few of these (social-) skills can be trained and learned. Most of the competences are given by nature and are part of the character and require authority to lead human beings.

A survey conducted by Gabriela Stahl revealed female executives' opinions and claimed advantages of their presences in top management positions in Germany. In their opinion there would be greater diversity of opinions at the top level companies can benefit from.

Speaking from experience, they stem from empathy, excellent communicative skills and an effective inclusion of other departments. Accordingly they create a better working atmosphere and reach a higher level of staff motivation.

Danna Jeschke also has a clear opinion on the features of female leaders: "From my experience women are very focused on good quality work, while men see much more value in networking, selling something which is not always theirs. Men waste too much time to pretend more and focus on what catches attention outside. Women are highly efficient and are focused on what makes things flow. Female leaders are better leaders because they really lead and like to show and take pride that other people really do good work." (Jeschke, 2012) The following quote completes the line of thoughts: "Women work for a project; men make sure it is well known." (Annies & Bongaerts, 2008)

A lot of the female leading attributes described are attempts to enhance staff's self-esteem and energizing them. Overall female managers belief that people execute best when they feel good about themselves and their work, and they generate opportunities that contribute to that. (Rosener, 2012)

On the other hand, the same female executives have a low determination and willingness to take risks and rather avoid rivalry and competition. (Stahl & Mühling, 2010) These male connoted characteristics are also relevant to being a good leader.

However, every leader needs to be willing to make unpopular and lonely decisions for the good of the company. The long and short of it is that there is no yes or no regarding the question if women are better leaders. Some skills male leaders scoop from easily, are more helpful to accomplish top leading positions. Relating to the difference theory, women are different from men, they have strengths that men do not have but they also have weaknesses, those men do not have and vice versa. (Henn, 2009)

First and foremost every person and every leadership style is different and the suitability also depends on the context the leader is working in. This assumption is solidified by Burns; saying that leaders evolve from a structure of motivation, values and goals. Therefore a mix of both male and female strengths in teams is preferable which is only possible when both, especially women, have an equal chance to reach the top management. This is why companies cannot miss out looking at a more diverse- female - pool of talent, which fits present global economic circumstances.

4. Status Quo in Germany & difficulties Women are facing

The compatibility of family and professional life in Germany is still difficult especially for women. A longitudinal analysis performed by the German Ministry of Family, Pensioners, Women and Youth shows that the phase of founding a family is a risk to a women's career but a chance for men to pursue a career.

81% of the women in leadership positions in Germany refrain from having children as a sacrifice for their career. Equally remarkable is the fact that women not only are a minority in management positions but also have a lower income than men in the same position. (Holst, 2008)

Year	2001	2002	2003	2004	2005	2006	2007	2008
Total number of Managers:	1.142	1.692	1.369	1.370	1.239	1.330	1.290	1.235
Therefrom Women:	251	387	312	303	273	315	323	314
Percentage	21%	22%	22%	22%	22%	23%	25%	25%

Graphic 2 – Executive Managers in Private Economy in Germany | Compare Holst 2008

The graphic shows very clearly how little progress has been made in eight years; only a four per cent increase was measured for women in executive management positions in Germany.

In 2010 Germany ranks eleventh with a share of 30,8% in general executive positions, which is below the EU average of 32,5%.

Thus women only claim a quarter of leadership spots in the private economy, the share of female members in executive boards is even poorer.

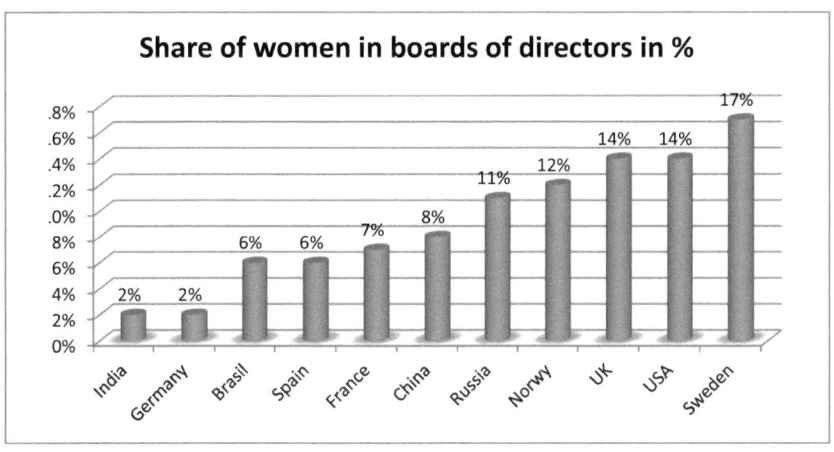

Graphic 3 – Share of women in boards of directors | Compare Kuerscher 2010

Only 49 women are member of the boardroom of Germanys 500 largest companies, which is an overall representation of only 2,4%. (Stahl & Mühling, 2010)

The correlation between both numbers underpins the assumption that there are neither enough female role models nor female recruiters in top positions to help women break the glass ceiling.

Asking Danna Jeschke why she thinks there are so little women in management positions, she says: "Because of perception and because the ones that judge if you are eligible are men. (...) Men like to support themselves, and others that are more like themselves." (Jeschke, 2012)

Stahl supports this opinion with the results of his study: "Women are often confronted with reservations about women in leadership (...) being the first and only woman in the board there was intense scrutiny and women were not granted the confidence or leap of faith that men often enjoy at comparable points in their career. (...) Prejudices against women and a lack of equal opportunity had hampered women's progress into top management." (Stahl & Mühling, 2010, p. 26) Wipperman calls congenially men "the guardians of the glass ceiling". Thus reputation of business in Germany is one of a boys club. (Wroe, 2011) Elke Holst adds findings of a study, which says that men have reservations against women due to traditions and their belief that female social labelling and top positions do not go well together. According to that study male managers also think that women find self-fulfilment in their private family life and therefore are not interested in climbing the career ladder. (Holst & Wiemer, 2010)

Danna Jeschke adds regarding external challenges: "(...) Mostly there are external challenges. For example equal partners do not recognize me as such because I am a woman. I am not perceived as being on the same level but rather a secretary or assistant." (Jeschke, 2012)

But recently this issue has also become more relevant for male employees. The national economy is in desperate need of higher birth rates but at the same time more qualified women entering the labour market.

Consequently both family members are struggling balancing work and life. This situation might prevent women from climbing the career ladder and rather take care of the family. This state is especially tragic because a lot is invested in women's education and they are known to accomplish better degrees than their fellow male students. It is, economically speaking, unprofitable to invest in the ones education without using the revenue or return on investment.

The Ministry of Family also concedes that working hours especially in leading positions are not compatible for women as well as family life and are dominated by male life designs: long hours and presence in the office. (Holst, 2008)

Danna Jeschke, Managing Director at a German University believes this is also a very German working behaviour: "Working long hours is very old fashioned and German. I think it's a perception thing (…) people think if you do not sit here 24 hours, you cannot be efficient. But I believe if you have to here 24 hours you are not efficient." (Jeschke, 2012)

In order to have more of these well-educated women entering management positions, sustainable restructuring of society and professional life is necessary as well as rethinking traditional gender stereotypes.

Wipperman's research also enumerates other reasons why competent women refrain from entering leadership positions. Mostly these women fear to have to perform better than men being equally employed and feeling a higher pressure of expectations. According to Wipperman, women also are afraid of defending their personal and mostly different management concepts against colleagues and subordinates but above all they perceive a problem in integrating job and family. (Wippermann, 2010) These results are supported by Danna Jeschke but come along with hope: "There were assumptions when I started: like she cannot be efficient because she has two kids and she has to leave early. You have to go through that and ignore it. This behaviour is very German; I did not experience that in any other country." (Jeschke, 2012)

This is why women who reach top positions put tremendously high pressure on themselves because they mirror on the success patterns of men and try to live up to these criteria. (Wessels, 2006)

In line with a more global labour market, there is the danger that good educated women could leave Germany looking for better career conditions. Alternatively women could change their career looking for other occupation not according to their potential and formal qualification. (Lindstädt, et al., 2011)

But there are attempts to change the situation for working parents in Germany. From January 2013 German families have the legal right to obtain a child care spot for children under three years of age. This law is a great success for men, women and families equally and is guaranteeing childcare to every child in Germany. Unfortunately the child-care-infrastructure is not ready for that law to be in effect. According to the statistical institute for youth, Germany is still missing 260.000 childcare spots. It is significant that the German government is trying to substitute childcare spots by introducing "Betreuungsgeld" (care money) at the beginning of 2013. (Holst & Schimeta, 2012) This money is supposed to be a substitute for the missing childcare spot and should prevent families from going to court. This care money will have the opposite effect from that intended by the law – rather than getting mothers to go back to work; they will stay at home caring for their children. This substitute would be an actual hindrance for women to get back into their profession as soon as possible and catch up on what has been missed. Absence from work does not help mothers pursue careers.

In order to understand the status quo in Germany a little better, but also adding a little polemic flavour to the discussion, the following statement of Joseph Ackermann former Head of the Deutsche Bank should not be left out: "Leading women are desirable because they make committees and offices more colourful." The answer to that statement by Silvana Koch-Mehrin German Politician and member of the European Parliament was:" If Mr Ackermann wants more colour on management boards, he should hang pictures on the wall." (Wroe, 2011)

5. Legal Aid called Women's Quota

44% of top female managers in Germany's 500 largest companies endorse the introduction of a mandatory women's quota. (Stahl & Mühling, 2010) So far, Germany has not implemented a legally binding women's quota. The issue of how to use the potential of women in leadership positions splits into two directions: either to have a legal binding quota in line with harsh sanctions, or having companies commit on a voluntary basis. At the least there does seem to be a common understanding of the economic need for more women in top management. A few German companies, one of them being Deutsche Telekom, have implemented a policy that by 2015, 30% of its middle and upper management positions have to be occupied by women. (Moore, 2010) Nevertheless, there are many opponents to the quota, emphasizing that companies must be free to choose the best managers regardless of sex. But will German company's act towards more women in leadership position unless they are forced to do so? Probably not! Self-set goals and admonishment by the government has not been fruitful. The percentage of women in top positions has not increased significantly. Danna Jeschke, when asked about the women quota, comments: "It is necessary and a good thing. Without it nothing will ever change otherwise." (Jeschke, 2012)

The strongest proponent of a women quota in Germany, Ursula von der Leyen makes it very clear: "According to the progress of the past ten years, which is only visible with a magnifying glass, a women quota needs to be implemented. A women quota of at least 30 per cent is the basis for negotiations. Crucial is the time period for implementation, it should be less years than I have fingers on my hand." (Kürschner, 2011, p. 74)

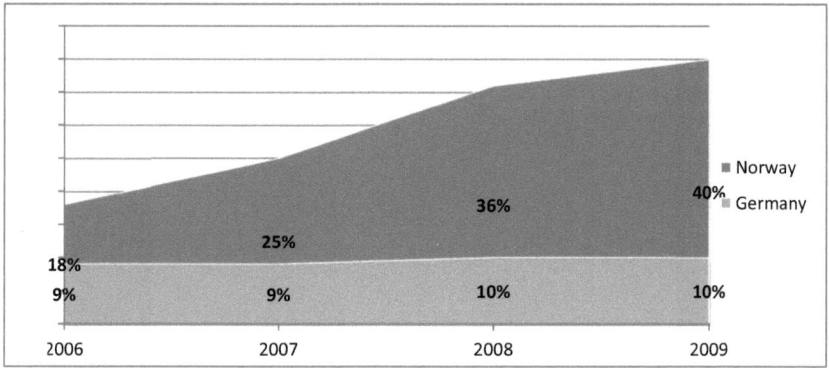

Graphic 4 - Development of women share in executive boards. Comparison of Norway & Germany | compare Kuerschner 2010

Norway is the first country in the world that introduced the women quota for all government owned companies as well as all companies listed on the stock exchange in 2003. When two years later not all required companies reached the quota of 40%, the government threatened those companies with dissolution. Today, all mandatory Norwegian companies meet the quota, which in 2012 even achieved 42%. (Storvik & Teigen, 2010) Since the introduction of the quota, the Norwegian economy also grew by two per cent on average and mastered the world financial recession like no other western country, because a new pool of talents was developed. (Kürschner, 2011)

Some qualitative evidence that quotas change attitudes in economy is presented by Pande:"(...) Female boards directors in Norway perceive themselves to have more influence, receive more information, and are more engaged in social interaction with the increased ratio of female board members after the quota law was implemented." (Pande & Deanne, 2011, p. 26)

However the successful implementation of the quota was primarily due to sanctions, which were in effect after four years of implementation.

Norway also facilitated women and companies with a database, where women could register with their CV and companies could search for talent. Additionally, Norwegian employers' associations created a "Female Future" training program, which were open for companies to send their employees to. (Storvik & Teigen, 2010) Until today the quota is broadly accepted in Norwegian economies, society and politics and also shows exemplary that without the quota legislation, there will be no change.

"Companies need women. And men need pressure. We must establish this now or we'll be sitting grey-haired in our wheelchairs before anything changes."
Petra Ledendecker, president of the Association of German Businesswomen

5.1. WOMEN QUOTA – ONLY FIGHTING THE SYMPTOM?

"Where there are statutory rules, there is progress." (Spiegel Online, 2012) According to Viviane Reding the quota would bring change. Sweden does not have a women's quota but is listed second in Europe regarding women in executive boards, 19% of all executive boards seats are held by Swedish women. (European-Commission, 2010)

However, Sweden has introduced other measures, which help women to combine work and family life that have proved extremely successful and effective. These measures consist of: tax cuts for households and childcare services as well as incentives for more fathers to take parental leave. (Moore, 2010)

Also the UK was successful with a voluntarily commitment for companies and increased the percentage of women in managerial positions within one year from 12,5% to 15%. (Holst & Schimeta, 2012)

Unfortunately the voluntary commitment in Germany was not successful and accompanying measures are still underdeveloped. Moreover, this problem is inevitably connected to business culture and social acceptance, both of which are deficient in Germany. Male monoculture dominates the picture and has to be forced to change. According to Danna Jeschke, the women quota is a must anticipating the following changes it will bring along: "the working atmosphere will change, leadership will change and performance will become more important than appearance. It's a win-win for society and companies. Once it is visible that women can do both; it will attract more women to follow the same career path. This gain creates a bigger pool of female mangers. You have to push it through, otherwise it never happens." (Jeschke, 2012)

The researchers Elke Holst and Julia Schimenta only anticipate a small path for companies to obviate the quota and skills shortage, which they sum up in five steps:

I.   Companies need to define a clear goal
II. Companies need to design a binding timeline and put it in traceable action
III. Companies need to have a transparent job advertisement and recruiting process
IV. Companies need to implement a human resource development that ensure integration of women and offers flexible career options
V.   Companies need to develop a women friendly culture. (Holst & Schimeta, 2012)

In line with Holst and Schimenta's conclusions, I asked Danna Jeschke if she sees other options for increasing the female percentage in management. She contemplates: "It will be harder. Management has to be more attractive for women. If it is more attractive and women feel appreciated and are able to combine private and professional life. Right now the male managers would not change anything: therefore we need the quota if we want to change something now." (Jeschke, 2012)

Also one needs to keep in mind that top management positions are always desired but also limited. Men are probably not keen on sharing those few spots and therefore maintain their negative attitude towards the quota.

Affirmative action or a quota for minorities is an effort to overcome prejudicial treatment and include minorities in the labour market. The European PWN Board Women Monitor also displays that women-only quotas drove the noteworthy increase in gender diversity on executive boards of companies in Europe. (Baldez, 2006) A quota would aim straight at the problem increasing the female share in management positions and would be allocating talented women in the labour market.

Pande explains the necessity for a women quota with an easy allegory: "For a healthy person, high doses of vitamin supplements may be unnecessary or even harmful, but for a person whose system is out of balance, supplements are an efficient way to restore the bodies balance." (Pande & Deanne, 2011, p. 30)

> *"I have passionately resisted any type of quota for a long time. However I have seen that appeals do not work and companies don't take voluntary action."*
> Ilse Aigner, German Minister for agriculture & consumer protection

5.2. PROS & CONS OF WOMEN'S QUOTA

The quota would be the legal vitamin for women striving to achieve more but being hindered to get there. A sizeable asset of the women quota is that in a majority of cases it would raise the self-esteem of women providing them with respectable positions and opportunities of advancement.

A quota would also set processes in motion that ensure a fairer recruitment procedure and development of women. "(…) A recent study of CEOs found that women leaders are more likely than men to promote other women into the highest ranks of the corporate hierarchy and therefore argues for affirmative action (…) more women in high-level managerial positions would also tend to have a substantial effect as role models." (Holst & Wiemer, 2010, p. 11)

Governmental stipulation would pace the change and set deadlines, while companies could concentrate implementing according measures and develop a professional culture.

Women would also be able to relax and grow as well as concentrate on their performance instead of fighting structural plus stereotypical hurdles.

Quotas are also a means of ensuring that teams maintain diverse in order to perform better and male monoculture is put to an end. Quota legislation emphasizes gender balance as a principle of justice and could be considered a positive discrimination approach to achieve gender equality.

Another essential advantage regarding the quota would be "choice". Women would automatically add to a bigger and more diverse assortment of recruitment choices, thus unseen talent could rise.

Baldaz also mentions that an initial critical mass is needed to give women more self-reliance in taking the floor. (Baldez, 2006)

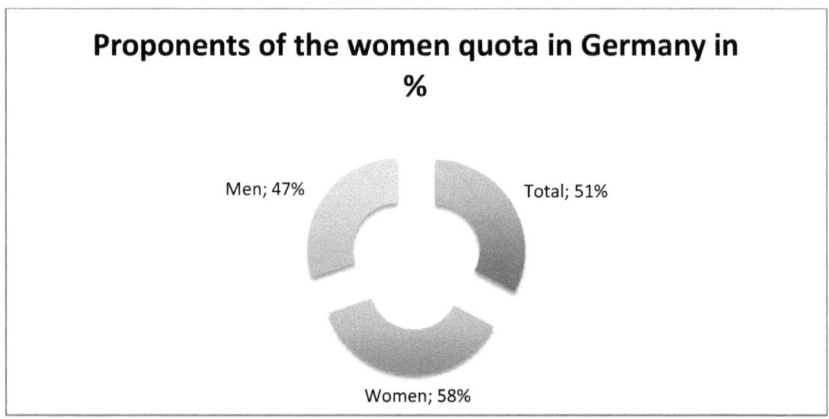

Graphic 5 – Proponents of the women quota in Germany | Compare Kuerschner

Another fundamental factor in favour of the quota is the creation of role models (the meaning and importance of role models - especially for women - will be elaborated in a following chapter). Thus a quota could improve and encourage women's investment in their own human capital and education when recognizing there is a real chance and opportunities to actually access top position. (Pande & Deanne, 2011)

There being a lot of opponents to the women quota, the following counter arguments concerning the women quota are voiced:

The main argument of adversaries is that an implementation of the quota would give the government too much political influence and intervention on economy, which would interfere with the efficient working of the market. When hiring a person you want the most qualified person available based on skills not affirmative action.

Companies also raised objections because foreign investors could be scared away by the quota regulation and governmental influence on the firm.

Moreover there is the fear that mediocre women will replace talented male leaders, which would mean losing skilled managers on the one hand but also fertilize a bad reputation for women receiving a top position due to the quota. Other voices claim that a women quota would not make sense since family and career cannot be unified. This is why the quota cannot be implemented alone but has to be flanked by other measures that allow the unification of career and private life. (Schupp, 2011) There is also the fear amongst women becoming "quota women" who only were granted a top position because of affirmative action and not because of their qualification and merit. Hence quotas could undermine women's credibility and depreciate the value of women, suggesting their success is only due to political influence on the company. Women are afraid to be reduced only to their gender and not according to past achievements and performance, being stigmatized through quota (Wippermann, 2010)

Other females are concerned about being victimized, implying that they are so weak that they need the quota. This perception could put men in the picture of a saviour – like, women and children first! (Schnatmeyer, 2003)

Finally there are lots of concerns the quota being discriminatory against men. Suspicions that this particular affirmative action could be a kick off for other marginalized ethics and minorities in society such as race, religion and age etc. to claim a quota exist. There is also a very practical concern on where to set the quota – how high or how low. Moreover sanctions and consequences for companies, which do not comply, are unclear and difficult to define. A generally valid quota would not take special needs or specifics of companies into account and should be differentiated by industrial sector. (Lindstädt, et al., 2011)

Finally, organization owners claim the right to decide who is employed and is represented in the executive boards, since they invest and risk their money. But on the other hand they also have a social responsibility towards their employees and society, participating in the country's economy in a fair and democratic manner.

Although there seem to be more con arguments, one point weighs the most: Nothing else seems to work. That is why the quota is needed. Women need policies, practice and social norms to change so that they have the same opportunities as men to fulfil multiple sets of values and orientations. (Holst, 2011)

According to Ursula Mueller the percentage of women in top positions has to exceed 15% and achieve a critical mass in order for change to be set in motion. (Müller, 1999)

5.3. ACCOMPANYING MEASURE FOR MORE WOMEN IN MANAGERIAL POSITIONS

So the question remains: What can be done to increase the percentage of women in leading positions? And how can the progress be accelerated and be more sustainable?

Germany is one of the European countries with fewer women working and having children. The mother-labour quota in Germany is 51% while Sweden's is 78%.

It is a prerequisite to have more women in gainful employment before them entering managerial sites. It is evident that if the percentage of women working is small, even fewer women will have the chance of leadership.

Noors findings punctuate the demand for additional measures helping women to cope: "In families with no children at home, the total workload for both men and women employed were 60 hours per week. For women, the number of hours per week increased rapidly with children at home. (...) Women's total workload was 90 hours, men's 70 hours per week." (Noor, 2002)

But some women need both professional success and private fulfilment to be happy. "I would say private success is more important but only if you have achieved a certain professional success. There needs to be a good balance." (Jeschke, 2012)

WORK-LIFE-BALANCE & CHILDCARE

The first idea that comes to mind is the compatibility of job and family: Upgrading childcare gives parents the possibility of working part- or full-time, and possibly enhancing their careers. It is particularly important that the German government ensures an excellent, comprehensive public child care system accessible to all citizens for any duration demanded. The government also needs to offer financial incentives, so women going to work and men staying at home are equally attractive than the most common opposite is now. This especially has implications on the German tax and social security system and the costs for childcare. Danna Jeschke adds: "It's a pain in Germany. Half of women's salaries go into childcare but you have to think long term, when the kids are grown up and live their own life, women still can continue work and their career without having to break and drop out of the labour market. For some years you might have a negative return, but it pays off in the long run." (Jeschke, 2012) If this basic measure is a given, additional provisions by the government and companies working together will be more successful. So far these measures only allow women to participate in the German labour market but are not extensive enough to enable women to pursue a career.

In additional to child care, companies also need to ensure a flexible and innovative working environment: home office, flexible working hours, job sharing, long-time work hour budgets, part time jobs also in managing positions and up to date technologies that make virtual meetings possible. Part-time work offers one way for women to reconcile family and professional life, but it also reduces the chances of reaching a top position. One should not exclude another. German companies need to abolish the compulsion for attendance and become more task oriented instead of time oriented.

The compatibility of work & career and (family)-life is getting extremely important for future employees, also known as Generation Y.

Men and women should have the chance to design their work-life balance more freely, meaning that taking off time for a sabbatical could help employees to focus on another phase of their life and develop despite work. The need for time off is very likely to occur in the future for German employees wanting to take care of high maintenance elderly family members. Thus taking care of family members besides children is something companies have to anticipate.

FAIR RECRUITMENT-, SELECTION-, APPLICATION- & TREATMENT PROCEDURES

Companies need to make sure that they have a "fair share" regarding their recruitment processes as well as sensitive sex sponsorship, fostering their talent pool and promotions. It is important to make provision for women and create equal chances right from the beginning as well as not to give statistical discrimination a chance. This could be done for all areas of a company by using "equality-controlling". HR processes need to be transparent and standardized. "I think companies have to be gender blind. Period. Whatever they do for men, they have to do for women. (...) That is the only thing that is going to work." (Ragins, et al., 1998)

These unbiased HR processes should also include a management by objective for all employees which would also obviate presence oriented working times common in Germany.

Besides those measures, it should be easier to enter companies from other branches and disciplines, which could help dealing with the lack of skilled talent and lower the bar for women who were not education in a certain field (e.g. technical education).

But most important, there is a realization of equal payment for the same job performance.

NETWORKING

A survey within British board members disclosed that 50% of them were recruited due to personal contacts, friendships and a widespread network. (Holst & Wiemer, 2010) Women also need to learn to use networking as a career tool. Gabriele Stahls study came up with 34% women naming a lack of existing professional networks as an obstacle to advancing female career. The study also showed that existing networks within companies are not adequately aimed at women's needs. On the other hand, women in that study also admitted that they find it difficult to use a professional network endorsing their own career. (Stahl & Mühling, 2010) A way to familiarize women with an instrument, which works well for men, is to formalize career networks for women. IBM for instance introduced monthly women network evenings, where female employees from all departments and hierarchy levels meet and exchange ideas, concerns etc. Those networks would not only help getting in touch with and learning from role models - fellow career ambitioned women - but also have a multiplication effect.

Nevertheless, women have to also learn do enhance their own marketing, work on their self-confidence and promote their skills - from being the helpful likable colleague to being a visible female role model.

MENTORS & FEMALE ROLE MODELS

"Women in higher ranked positions are role models for other women." (Holst, 2006, p. 43) It is very important for women to have somebody their own gender to look up to and to see that it works. Positive role models can have a snowball effect, change company's norms and provide a greater variety of leadership styles. Danna Jeschke emphasizes the need for female role models: "Role models are the most important thing. You have to see that it is working. Even when I have doubts, I see other women having kids and working and I think they can do it, so I can as well. (…)" (Jeschke, 2012)

Studies indicated that a high share of qualified women in top positions has a positive effect on the promotion of more women. (Holst & Wiemer, 2010) While men have countless role models to choose from, women only have a small group to select, identify with and share concerns as well as common experience.

"(…) I think mentors make sense if they have the power to help you." (Jeschke, 2012) An interview conducted by Ragins concludes the importance of mentors: "Mentors are the single most critical piece to women advancing career-wise. In my experience you need somebody to help guide you and go to bat for you. (…) I am saying, because you are a woman, you need somebody to fight some of your battles in the male environment. (…) Mentors will help you reinforce the decisions that are made with others, help you understand the organization, understand the players and to understand the personalities. (…)" (Ragins, et al., 1998, p. 32) According to Ragins, employees with mentors receive more promotions, have more career mobility and advance at a faster rate than those lacking mentors. (Ragins, et al., 1998)

Thus mentoring could be a particularly helpful tool especially for women aiming at the glass ceiling.

LEAVE OF ABSENCE

As a matter of their own interest, companies should encourage programs that smooth transitions before, during and after parental leave. Companies need to prevent women from losing track of their job by accompanying women during maternity leave, helping them to get back into the job fast and adapting to changes that might have occurred during their leave of absence. Deutsche Telekom for instance implemented a "stay in contact" program, helping women managers to keep in touch with the office while on maternity leave. A permanent mentor can also embody this role, helping women to achieve. (Bundesregierung, 2006) (Wirth, 2004) (Guenther & Gerstenmaier, 2005)

COACHING & AWARENESS TRAINING

Equally important when training women to succeed in management positions, it is essential to find out where discrimination and prejudices within a company still exist. Awareness trainings can help identifying those key factors helping women to reach higher positions and being accepted by subordinates. (Schnatmeyer, 2003)

Conflict management seminars could also be necessary and help staff coping with diversity and the issues it could create.

PROFESSIONAL CULTURE & COMMITMENT

The highest level of management carries out the most important role regarding this subject. Only if equal treatment and advancement of women in leadership position are understood, desired, accepted, enforced and supported will it become part of the company's culture. A cultural revolution like this entails the full and visible commitment of the company's heads and senior management.

Therefore diversity awareness training would be advisable, since it could help to create an environment where both women and men can blossom.

Rindfleisch suggests including financial bonuses as a reward for enacting change policies and building activities changing organizational structure into executive's performance criteria. (Rindfleish & Sheridan, 2003)

An equally huge part regarding this issue is to get society to give moral support to women and diminish female stereotypes. Career women must become an accepted and normal part of everyday life in Germany. The promotion of a positive image of working- and career woman is key.

Companies' obligations towards women should also be included in the annual report, giving a yearly overview of women related management ratios and indicators.

To put it in a nutshell, there are four principal aspects of having more women in managerial positions: I. Create awareness in society, II. Develop a new corporate culture, III. Implement a modern human resources management and IV. Improve the compatibility of job and family.

CERTIFICATION

Recently, certificates play a greater role for companies. There are certifications or audits for work life balance, quality, sustainability, ecological friendly production - why not for equal treatment of men and women in the work context? Commonly accepted certification could put pressure on companies and increase their self-regulation. It is also getting more common for future employees to look at evaluation website like KUNUNU.de for more insights on their future employer. Positive feedback in those online platforms as well as certification could be orientation help for graduates finding their prospective employer.

FURTHERANCE OF MEN

One might wonder if the only approach that helps women into managerial positions is only by supporting women. However, another approach could be to literally familiarise men with another role. The same stereotype problem that applies to women also applies to men being the breadwinner of the family following his career. Men also have to recognise an additional path in their lives and go for it. More and more men are also interested in spending time with their family and even taking time off to spend quality time with the kids. This rising interest goes along well with women's attempts to achieve more. Judy Rosener found that just as many men as women experience a work-family conflict, especially with children in the family. (Rosener, 2012)

Therefore companies, colleagues and society need to be more understanding, accepting and create an environment that shows men that it is fine to have other goals in life besides career. Measures to achieve these aims could be: flexible working hours and possibilities to obtain a part time job without the obstacles of getting promoted. It is also pre-eminent that it becomes normal for men to take parental leave without being laughed at by colleagues and expecting disadvantages for continuity of work. Thus the development of women can also happen with a development of men.

SOCIETY

As mentioned before, society plays a big role in this context, especially the German culture of presence at work. People need to move away from the impression and conviction that people who work most and longest have the most meaningful position. Companies and society need to think more goal-oriented, leaving individuals the liberty designing their own professional sequence apart from society's framework. Danna Jeschke cuts to the chase: "More awareness for this issue needs to be created!" (Jeschke, 2012)

> *„If a woman, who stands behind a successful man, wants to proceed, she has to turn her back on him."*
> *Maria Sukop, Mother & Poet*

Apart from the measures that are required by companies, government and society, an immense amount needs to be understood by women in order to reach top positions. Women need to be convinced that they can succeed and that they have the ability to fill top management positions.

In order to get there, they have to demand professional progression and ask for the same chances as men unrelated to the implementation of the quota. Women need to step out of their shadow, present their talent and own initiative and engage in highly visible assignments. But they also need to be aware and accepting of failure and disappointment.

34

Most importantly and stated numerous times throughout the thesis: it is for women to create their own style because that is what fills the void.

> *"I am optimistic that resistance to the quota is diminishing. Awareness is growing that it would help companies change their internal culture."*
> Margarete Haase, CFO of Deutz engine construction

5.4. THE RIGHT WAY FOR GERMANY

The quota has been a highly controversial subject in Germany for a few years now. Neither politicians nor companies have found common ground for a solution.

In my opinion, there has to be a women's quota soon, otherwise there will not be enough pressure on companies to act. One modification should be made, which would also make the process/project more feasible. The quota should be reduced to executive boards.

"Finally, data shows that companies with women CEOs have more women on their boards and on their management teams than average. Taking this into account we can argue that quotas only need to be set for the top echelons, as change there will impact changes throughout the company." (Cons, 2005, p. 88) This means a separation of operative management and the supervisory board's level in terms of affirmative action. Only a few women at the top are enough to recruit and enhance further women in leadership positions and top management. This restraint would also be easier to push forward anytime soon and receive more support from companies. But it does not change the fact that there are still too few women in management positions.

Nevertheless additional political, legal, sociological and communication measures (as mentioned in previous chapters) are needed to prepare for women to have a sustainable future within lower and top management. Those means would also help to overcome the existing persistent stereotypes and behaviour patterns/structures existing in many German's minds. This mentality puts a lot of pressure on working mothers and fathers and does more harm than anticipated.

Finally, since the term "women quota" is not accepted by all participants and conveys the wrong message. It should not be used, since it implies a preferential advancement of women, which has a negative connotation. All women want is equality and equivalent chances to men.

6. Critical approach

First and foremost, the term 'women quota' gives a lot of room for criticism. In my opinion it does not help women to be taken seriously but rather feel like an aid project instead of competent professionals. That is why the political measures should not be called 'women quota' but maybe just indicate that an equal share of both men and women have to be present in boards. This would maybe also increase the acceptance of political involvement towards economy and take the focus away from female labour.

Moreover, it should be observed critically that merely the quota seems to be of media importance but necessary aid that supports such affirmative action is almost never mentioned. Especially politicians seem to be looking for a quick win, regardless of the feasibility of the quota. Society should deliberately be made aware of the need for measures and given the chance to adjust to smaller steps. Especially daily news and the media play an important role regarding the issue. I dare say that maybe not everybody is aware of the consequences a waiver of female potential could have or what impact needs to be anticipated introducing a women quota. It would be sad to see such an important mission as just a politician's achievement during a single legislation period.

There is also the danger that the quota could leave women powerless and turn them into tokens, unless the initiative is followed up by measures and support. Women in leadership positions could be reached with the measurement mentioned in the previous chapters but for that to be evaluated, long term studies about measure effects would be necessary.

Another thought that comes to mind, looking at the quota critically, is that it does not make sense for all branches. Some industrial areas have to rely on men because not enough qualified women would be available due to their former education.

Besides the quota is a very rational, quantitative tool, which could leave a board with only one woman. This situation could prove to be very complicated and not helpful to both the acceptance of men and the success of the women.

It is very worrying that some women themselves reject the attempt for affirmative action, which is supposed to be helping them. This being the case, it is doubtful if it can succeed when missing the basics. Only the partial refusal can be very demoralizing for other women –moral support among women is a key factor in succeeding.

Before researching this topic and beginning this thesis, these opposing arguments came very easily and are still true. But during the reading and working process, tiny arguments and statements changed my mind. A quota would temporarily speed up the necessary change in thinking and get things moving more quickly.

> *"The fight against the quota is the final stand of a patriarchal society from the last century.*
> *The quota has been good for the Greens."*
> *Claudia Roth, co-leader of Germany's Green Party*

6.1. FUTURE OUTLOOK & ADVANTAGES FOR COMPANIES

It became very clear throughout the thesis that companies cannot proceed without using the potential of highly qualified women. The main reason for this is the demographic change but also the inevitability of institutionalising a plurality of talents and perspectives on management issues. Thus a company's strategic intelligence requires diversity. Diverse perspectives are protective armour that helps to avoid strategic mistakes. Another essential instrument for companies are mixed management teams, which assure swift reaction to changing situations.

A Catalyst study also found that companies with a higher number of women in boards had a higher financial success than companies with a lesser share of women in boards. The same study also identified that companies with an increasing percentage of women also increase their innovative performance. (Holst & Wiemer, 2010) These finding are reinforced by McKinsey, showing that diversity in boards – especially the visible presence of women – is an important factor for economic success. The reason for that success is differentiated discussions, risk aware decision making processes, balance decisions and a better control of the company. Women bring a fresh breeze, different approaches and ways of thinking that affect the climate of an organization. Diversity has a positive impact on companies performance overall. (Kommission, 2011) "It has also been shown that executive and supervisory boards with a higher percentage of women tend to make better use of existing company and market potentials. (...) Finally, a stronger representation of women on supervisory boards also provides added legitimacy for decisions in the eyes of employees, customers, investors, clients, and the public." (Holst & Schimeta, 2012, p. 26)

As mentioned before, women achieve the same educational degrees and are proven to be higher qualified than men. It is only therefore wise for companies to make use of these young female professionals. (Wippermann, 2010)

Implementing family-aware human-resource policies and ensuring that more women get into leadership positions has proven to have a positive impact on companies.

The study "Women Matter" by McKinsey states that companies investing in women and having a higher percentage of managing women gained 48% more profits than the average in the same branch. The study correspondingly implies that not only a single woman nor the alibi women can have impact, but that companies are most successful with a culture of diversity and mixed teams. (McKinsey, 2008)

Some of these effects are: higher working satisfaction and productivity of both male and female employees.

Moreover, studies have shown that women who feel supported by their company developed a sustainable bond. Thus companies gained loyalty as well low staff turnover. (Henn, 2009) According to Schnattmeyer, it is striking that monoculture organizations are more expensive than multicultural or diverse working environments. Thus diverse companies save money due to higher satisfaction, motivation, productivity in diverse firms as well as their effort towards employer branding.

The final advantage for companies employing more women in managerial positions is publicity. Public image is an essential aspect these days. Certification for CSR, sustainability as well as diversity is getting a huge factor for stakeholders. It is not merely price management that is key for gaining customers, partners and collaborators but also business culture.

"It must be in the interest of every company to create a top managerial body that is as diverse as possible, as the positive effects on the atmosphere, on staff loyalty, on the image and last but not least on the company earnings have been attested to many time." (Stahl & Mühling, 2010, p. 1)

„Emancipation will only be accomplished, if an incapable woman has moved to a responsible position."

Heidi Kabel, German Actress & Author

6.2. SUMMARY

The pressing issue in this context is securing the welfare of the German state and keeping the German economy running. An elderly population combined with decreasing birth rates endangers that welfare. Therefore it is crucial to make use of all the skilled human resources the country has to offer, i.e. women, in order to stay competitive as a leading economy.

Unfortunately, most women refrain from taking over leadership positions and still take the responsibility for domestic and family matters. The other side of the coin shows women who would like to enter the "boys club" but are hindered by the glass ceiling and society's constraints.

As previous chapters showed, prejudice and stereotypical dogma about a women's role in society still restrict their chances of reaching top positions in management.

My first research question was: *Is there a leadership style that differentiates men and women?* This question was based on the theoretical execution of transformational and transactions leadership styles. Yet, a final answer was not found since both men and women bear characteristics of both styles, while women leaders have more similarities with the transformational styles.

Nevertheless men and women do have different leadership skills that are both beneficial for companies and in my opinion a mix of both leaders set is promising. In my view it is also hard to distinguish and find a black and white answer, since the leadership style no matter who performs it, also depends on the branch, department, economic situation and mostly subordinates. I also believe that there are not enough reliable sources to make a final statement because the problems remain the same: not enough women in leadership position, therefore too few examples to observe. Since there is hope that the balance of men and women in management positions will improve, there will probably be more studies and observations regarding this question of different styles.

I also shy away of subscribing men and women a specific style because it would create stereotypes. And as was learned in this paper, stereotypes are one cause for the problem and cause for many assumptions that hinder equality.

This thought leads towards the next research question: *Why are there fewer women in top managerial positions in Germany?* The reasons for that have shown to be manifold. One reason is rooted in the German understanding of a women's role in society, which is more domesticated. This perception goes along with a very feminine stereotype that has never been shaken off. Consequently a lot of men do not believe in the concept of women being top managers and many women think they cannot succeed. Hence women are unaccounted for in many top positions.

A more structural reason is the missing organizational support for women and families in terms of childcare and more flexible working schedules. Both mentality and insufficient working infrastructure seems to be hindrance enough for women not to pursue their careers.

I assume that modern fathers being male managers will get an eye for the issue because they have well educated daughters who face the same challenges women do presently. They will also want their daughters, after investing a lot in their education, to succeed and be able to combine child and career.

The third research question was aiming at flanking measures: *Are there certain measures that help women to break through the glass ceiling?* In my view companies and government can assist a lot as outlined in a previous chapter.

In believe that flexible working conditions as well as guaranteed child-care would bring quick wins. Those measures have to outweigh the drawback, as some women see it, of being able to have children. Although the country needs higher birth rates, it is dependent on women who have their own conception of professional life.

The increase of women's participation should be part of Corporate Social Responsibility aims of each company in their own interest and as responsibility and moral action towards society. These targets need to be included in company's strategic plans and achievements should be disclosed in annual reports.

Mixed teams will contribute to the diversity of opinion and perspectives in management. Policies aligned with that understanding would help avoid risks and grasp chances in a globalized and complex world economy.

Unfortunately not all additional measures will bring quick wins, but women expect and the country needs a fast change. Therefore a legal binding quota is inevitable.

The final question was regarding the quota itself: *Is the women's quota the most sustainable way to get more women in top leadership positions in Germany?* In my personal opinion the quota is more sustainable and stable as part of a whole package of measures. Bringing more women into leadership positions is not merely a quantitative issue, which can be dictated by a law. Flanking measures are crucial to create an awareness as well as aid for women to succeed once being placed in top positions through the quota. Also high-level commitment is essential to change the existing culture within a firm, organization and society. Programs are needed to advance the presence of female role models and mentors already in the academic education hierarchy in order to help young females to shape their career aspirations accordingly.

Germany correspondingly needs to overcome still significant earning gaps between women and men, which can also be sourced back to that the women's high level of education is not reflected in the position they occupy in the labour market.

Lastly employers need to recognize the benefits women and diversity in general can bring to their businesses.

The Norwegian experience shows that there has to be an initial kick-off for something to change:

"I used to be very critical of quotas, but today, after experiencing the changes going on in business life and corporate boards in particular, it is now clear to me that this was an important and necessary move." (Storvik & Teigen, 2010, p. 11)

7. Appendix II – List of Diagrams | Figures | Tables

- **Graphic 1** – Characteristics of a Transformational Leader, page 12 | Compare Bass, Bernard, From transactional to transformation leadership. Learning to share the vision, 2006
- **Graphic 2** – Executive Managers in Private Economy in Germany, page 20 | Compare Holst, Elke, Führungskräfte Monitor 2001-2006. Berlin: DIW Berlin, 2008
- **Graphic 3** – Share of women in boards of directors | Compare Kürschner, Isabelle Die Quote - Kulturrevolution in der Arbeitswelt? München: Politische Studien - Hanns Seidel Stiftung, 2011
- **Graphic 4** - Development of women share in executive boards, page 21. Comparison of Norway & Germany, page 24 | compare Kürschner, Isabelle Die Quote - Kulturrevolution in der Arbeitswelt? München: Politische Studien - Hanns Seidel Stiftung, 2011
- **Graphic 5** - Proponents of the women quota in Germany, page 28 | compare Kürschner, Isabelle Die Quote - Kulturrevolution in der Arbeitswelt? München: Politische Studien - Hanns Seidel Stiftung, 2011

8. LITERATURE

- Ahern, K. & Dittmar, A., 2011. *The Changing og the Boards: The Impact on Form Valuation of Mandated Female Board Representation.* USA: University of Michigan.
- Annies, S. & Bongaerts, K., 2008. *Ausgebremst? Warum die Karriereleiter fuer Frauen oft zu kurz ist.* Berlin: Bertelsmann Stiftung.
- Baldez, L., 2006. The Pros and Cons of Gender Quota Laws: What Happens when you Kick Men Out and Let Women In?. *Politics & Gender,* Vol. 2(No. 1), pp. 102-128.
- Bass, B. M., 2006. *From transactional to transformational leadership: Learning to share the vision,* USA: Lawrence Erlbaum.
- Bhavnani, R., 2009. Do Electoral Quoatas Work after They Are Withdrawn? Evidence from a Natural Experiment in India. *American Political Science Review,* Vol. 103(No. 1), pp. 23-35.
- Bolder, R., Gosling, J., Marturano, A. & Dennison, P., 2003. *A review of Leadership Theory and Competency Frameworks.* Exeter: Centre for Leadership Studies University of Exeter.
- Bono, J. & Judge, T., 2004. Personality and Transformational and Transactional Leadership: A Meta Analysis. *Journal of Applied Psychology,* Vol. 89(No. 5), pp. 901-910.
- Bundesregierung, 2006. *2. Bilanz Chancengleichheit - Frauen in Fuehrungspositionen,* Berlin: s.n.
- Chen, L.-J., 2010. Do Gender Quotas Influence Womens Representation and Policies?. *The European Journal of Comparative Economics,* pp. Vol 7 Iss 1 pp 13-60.
- Conger, J. A., 1999. Charismatic and Transformational Leadership in Organizations: An Insiders Perspective on these Developing Stremas of Research. *Leadership Quarterly,* Vol. 10(No. 2), pp. 145-179.
- Cons, Q. P. a., 2005. NK. *Women@Work,* Volume No. 8, pp. 84-89.
- Dahlerup, D. & Freidenvall, L., 2005. Quotas as a Fast Track to Equal Reprentation for Women - Why Scandinavia is no longer the model. *International Feminist Journal of Politics,* Vol. 7(No. 1), pp. 26-48.
- Druskat, V. U., 1994. Gender and Leadership Style: Transformational and Transactional Leadership in the Roman Catholic Church. *Leadership Quaterly,* 5.pp. V 5 I 2 pp 99-119.
- Eagly, A. & Carli, L., 2003. The female leadership advantage: An evaluation of the evidence. *The Leadership Quarterly,* pp. 807-834.
- Eagly, A. & Johannesen-Schmidt, M., 2001. The Leadership Styles of Women and Men. *Journal of Social Issues,* 22 6.
- Eagly, A. & Johnson, B., 1990. *Gender and Leadership Style: A Meta Analysis.* University of Conneticut - Center for Health, Intervention and Prevention: CHIP Documents.

- European-Commission, 2010. *More women in senior positions. Key to economic stability and growth.,* Luxenburg: European Commission.
- Goddard, R., 2011. The case against the UKs affirmative action quotas for women on corporate boards. *Stephen Bainbridges Journal of Law, Politics and Culture.*
- Graw-Hill, M., 2003. Ten myths about affirmative action. *Journal of Social Issues,* pp. V 52 pp 25-31.
- Guenther, S. & Gerstenmaier, J., 2005. *Fuehrungsfrauen im Management: Erfolgsmerkmale und Barrieren ihrer Berufslaufbahn,* Muenchen: LMU.
- Hall, J., Johnson, S., Wysocki, A. & Kepner, K., 2008. *Transformational Leadership: The Transformation of Managers and Associates.* s.l.:University of Florida/ IFAS Extension.
- Hay, I., 2011. *Transformational Leadership: Characteristics and Criticisms.* Flinders University: School of Geography, Population and Enviromental Management.
- Henn, M., 2009. *Die Kunst des Aufstiegs.* Bonn: Bundeszentrale für politische Bildung.
- Hollmann, D., Annies, S. & Bongaerts, K., 2008. *Ausgebremst? Warum die KArriereleiter für Frauen oft zu kurz ist,* Berlin: Bertelsmann Stiftung.
- Holst, D. E., 2011. *Statement PD,* Berlin: DIS Berlin/Universität Flensburg.
- Holst, E., 2006. *Women in Managerial Positions in Europe: Focus on Germany,* Berlin: DIW Berlin.
- Holst, E., 2008. *Führungskräfte Monitor 2001-2006.* Berlin: DIW Berlin.
- Holst, E. & Schimeta, J., 2011. *Weekly Report: Twenty-nine women to 906 men: Continuing gender inequality on the boards of Germany top Companies,* Berlin: DIW Berlin.
- Holst, E. & Schimeta, J., 2012. *Top-Level Management in Large Companies: Persistent Male-Dominated Structures Leave Little Room for Women,* Berlin: DIW Berlin.
- Holst, E. & Wiemer, A., 2010. *Zur Unterrepräsentanz von Frauen in Spitzengremien der Wirtschaft Ursachen und Handlungsansätze,* Berlin: DIW Berlin.
- Hübler, O. & Menkhoff, L., 2010. *Do women manage smaller funds?.* Hannover: Leibniz Universität Hannover.
- Jeschke, D., 2012. *Interview* [Interview] (23 6 2012).
- Kommission, E., 2011. *Grünbuch: Europäischer Corporate Governance Rahmen,* Brüssel: Europäische Kommission.
- Kürschner, I., 2011. *Die Quote - Kulturrevolution in der Arbeitswelt?,* München: Politische Studien - Hanns Seidel Stiftung.
- Lindstädt, H., Wolff, M. & Fehre, K., 2011. *Frauen in Führungspositionen - Auswirkungen auf den Unternehmenserfolg.* Berlin: Bundesministerium für Familie, Senioren, Frauen und Jugend.

- MacGregor Burns, J., 2003. *Transforming Leadership: The Pursuit of Happiness,* USA: The Atlantic Press.
- McKinsey, 2007. *A Wake-Up Call for Female Leadership in Europe.* Berlin: McKinsey & Company.
- McKinsey, 2008. *Women Matter - Female leadership, a competitive edge for the future,* France: McKinsey & Company.
- Moore, T., 2010. *In germany, a quota for female managers.* Berlin: Time Magazine.
- Müller, U., 1999. Zwischen Licht und Grauzone: Frauen in Fühungspositionen. *Arbeit,* pp. Heft 2, Jg. 8, S. 137-161.
- NK, 2010. *Deutschland fällt bei Frauen Gleichstellung zurück.* [Online] Available at: www.spiegel.de [Accessed 2 5 2012].
- NK, 2010. *Fachkräftesicherung: Ziele und Maßnahmen der bundesregierung,* s.l.: Bundesministerium für Arbeit und Soziales.
- NK, 2010. *Women at the top of corporations: Making it happen,* Munich: McKinsey.
- NK, 2011. *Women in the boardroom: A global perspective,* s.l.: Deloitte.
- NK, 2012. *EU Kommisarin favorisiert Frauenquote für Europa.* [Online] Available at: www.spiegel.de [Accessed 5 3 2012].
- Noor, N., 2002. Work-Family Conflict, Locus of Control, and Womens Well Being: Test of Alternative Pathways. *The Journal of Social Psychology,* Vol. 142(No. 5), pp. 645-662.
- Pande, R. & Deanne, F., 2011. *Gender Quotas and Female Leadership,* NK: World Developement Report.
- Ragins, B. R., Townsend, B. & Mattis, M., 1998. Gender gap in the executive suite: CEOs and female executives report on breaking the glass ceiling. *Academy of Management Executive,* pp. Vol 12 No 1 pp 28-42.
- Rindfleish, J. & Sheridan, A., 2003. Women in Management Review: No change from within: senior women managers resonse to gendered organizational structures. *Emerald,* pp. Vol 18 Iss 6 pp. 299-310.
- Rosener, J., 2012. Ways Women Lead. *Harvard Business Review,* Issue retrieved - 11.07.2012.
- Sanders, J., Hopkins, W. & Geroy, G., 2003. From Transactional to Transcendental: Toward an Integrated Theory of Leadership. *Journal of Leadership & Organizational Studies,* Vol. 9(No. 21).
- Schnatmeyer, D., 2003. *Frauen und Führung: Berufliche Segregation und neue Konzepte zur Chancengleichheit,* s.l.: DIE.
- Schupp, J., 2011. *Fuehrt eine Frauenquote zu mehr Gerechtigkeit?,* Berlin: s.n.
- Spiegel Online, 2012. *www.spiegel.de.* [Online] Available at: www.spiegel.de/wirtschaft/soziales/01518 [Accessed 1 6 2012].

- Stahl, G. & Mühling, N., 2010. *Germanys female executives call introduction of women's quota helpful,* Frankfurt: Odgers Berndtson.
- Stewart, J., 2006. Transformational Leadership: An evolving concept examined through the works of Burns, Bass, Avolio and Leithwood. *Canadian Journal of Educational Administration and Policy,* p. Issue 54.
- Storvik, A. & Teigen, M., 2010. *Women on Board - The Norwegian Experience,* Berlin: Friedrich Ebert Stiftung.
- Terjesen, S. & Singh, V., 2008. Female presence on corporate boards: A multi country study of enviromental context. *Journal of Business Ethics,* pp. V 83 N 1 pp 55-63.
- Thornton, G., 2012. *Women in senior management: still not enough,* s.l.: s.n.
- Trzcinski, E. & Holst, E., 2010. *Gender Differences in Subjective Well-Being in and out of Management Positions,* Berlin: DIW Berlin.
- Wessels, D., 2006. *www.karrierefuehrer.de.* [Online]
Available at: www.karrierefuehrer.de
[Accessed 1 6 2012].
- Wippermann, C., 2010. *Women in Executive Positions - Barriers and Bridges,* Heidelberg: Federal Ministry for Family Affairs, Senior Citizens, Women and Youth, Survey by Sinus Sociovision.
- Wirth, L., 2004. *Breaking through the glass ceiling - Women in Management,* Geneva: s.n.
- Wroe, D., 2011. *Do Germans need a gender quota?.* [Online]
Available at: www.globalpost.com/print?564684
[Accessed 2 4 2012].
- Yukl, G., 1989. *Managerial Leadership: A Review of Theory and Research.* New York: Journal of Management.